Jim Burns's work represents his integrity, intelligence, and his heart for kids. The *Uncommon* high school group studies will change some lives and save many others.

stephen arterburn
Bestselling Author, *Every Man's Battle*

Jim Burns knows kids, understands kids and _____
youth workers, both volunteer and professional, can use.

ridge burns
President, God's Kids (www.godskids.org)

Jim Burns has found the right balance between learning God's Word and applying it to life. The topics are relevant, up to date and on target. Jim gets kids to think. This is a terrific series, and I highly recommend it.

les j. christie
Chair of Youth Ministry, William Jessup University, Rocklin, California

There are very few people in the world who know how to communicate life-changing truth effectively to teens. Jim Burns is one of the best. These studies are biblically sound, hands-on practical and just plain fun. This one gets a five-star endorsement.

ken davis
Author and Speaker (www.kendavis.com)

I don't know anyone who knows and understands the needs of the youth worker like Jim Burns. The *Uncommon* high school group studies are solid, easy to use and get students out of their seats and into the Word.

doug fields
President, Simply Youth Ministry (www.simplyyouthministry.com)

The practicing youth worker always needs more ammunition. The *Uncommon* high school group studies will get that blank stare off the faces of the kids at your youth meeting!

jay kesler
President Emeritus, Taylor University, Upland, Indiana

In the *Uncommon* high school group studies, Jim Burns pulls together the key ingredients for an effective series. He captures the combination of teen involvement and a solid biblical perspective with topics that are relevant and straightforward. This will be a valuable tool in the local church.

dennis "tiger" mcluen
Executive Director, Youth Leadership (www.youthleadership.com)

Young people need the information necessary to make wise decisions related to everyday problems. The *Uncommon* high school group studies will help many young people integrate their faith into everyday life, which, after all, is our goal as youth workers.

miles mcpherson
Senior Pastor, The Rock Church, San Diego, California

This is a resource that is user-friendly, learner-centered and intentionally biblical. I love having a resource like this that I can recommend to youth ministry volunteers and professionals.

duffy robbins
Professor of Youth Ministry, Eastern University, St. Davids, Pennsylvania

The *Uncommon* high school group studies provide the motivation and information for leaders and the types of experience and content that will capture high school people. I recommend it highly.

denny rydberg
President, Young Life (www.younglife.org)

Jim Burns has done it again! This is a practical, timely and reality-based resource for equipping teens to live life in the fast-paced, pressure-packed adolescent world of today.

rich van pelt
President, Alongside Consulting, Denver, Colorado

Jim Burns has his finger on the pulse of youth today. He understands their mindsets and has prepared these studies in a way that will capture their attention and lead them to greater maturity in Christ.

rick warren
Senior Pastor, Saddleback Church, Lake Forest, California
Author of *The Purpose Driven Life*

jim burns

general editor

the old
testament

Published by Gospel Light
Ventura, California, U.S.A.
www.gospellight.com
Printed in the U.S.A.

Originally published as *The Word on the Old Testament*
by Gospel Light in 1996.

Library of Congress Cataloging-in-Publication Data
The Old Testament / Jim Burns, general editor.
p. cm. — (Uncommon high school group study)
Previously published: The Word on The Old Testament, 1996.
Includes bibliographical references and index.
ISBN 978-0-8307-5645-2 (trade paper : alk. paper)
1. Bible. O.T.—Study and teaching. I. Word on the Old Testament.
BS1193.O37 2010
221.6071'2—dc22
2010035218

2 3 4 5 6 7 8 9 10 11 12 13 14 15 16 / 20 19 18 17 16 15 14 13 12 11

Rights for publishing this book outside the U.S.A. or in non-English languages are
administered by Gospel Light Worldwide, an international not-for-profit ministry.
For additional information, please visit www.glww.org, e-mail info@glww.org, or write
to Gospel Light Worldwide, 1957 Eastman Avenue, Ventura, CA 93003, U.S.A.

To order copies of this book and other Gospel Light products in bulk quantities,
please contact us at 1-800-446-7735.

dedication

This book was originally written by one of my youth ministry heroes, Kara Powell. Kara has done so much good as one of the foremost leaders in the field of youth ministry. I am so glad that Gospel Light has brought back and adapted this wonderful curriculum from Kara. It is the best Old Testament curriculum for kids I have ever seen.

Jim Burns

To the person I repect the most is the whole world: my mom. You taught me by your words and your example that when God calls, He always equips and provides. It is largely your prayers that strengthen and guide me. I count it an honor when people say I remind them of you!

Kara Powell

contents

how to use the *uncommon* group bible studies

Each *Uncommon* group Bible study contains 12 sessions, which are divided into 3 stand-alone units of 4 sessions each. You may choose to teach all 12 sessions consecutively, to use just one unit, or to present individual sessions. You know your group, so do what works best for you and your students.

This is your leader's guidebook for teaching your group. Electronic files (in PDF format) of each session's student handouts are available for download at **www.gospellight.com/uncommon/the_old_testament.zip**. The handouts include the "message," "dig," "apply," "reflect" and "meditation" sections of each study and have been formatted for easy printing. You may print as many copies as you need for your group.

Each session opens with a devotional meditation written for you, the youth leader. As hectic and trying as youth work is much of the time, it's important never to neglect your interior life. Use the devotions to refocus your heart and prepare yourself to share with kids the message that has already taken root in you. Each of the 12 sessions are divided into the following sections:

starter

Young people will stay in your youth group if they feel comfortable and make friends in the group. This section is designed for you and the students to get to know each other better.

message

The message section will introduce the Scripture reading for the session and get students thinking about how the passage applies to their lives.

dig

Many young people are biblically illiterate. In this section, students will dig into the Word of God and will begin to interact on a personal level with the concepts.

apply

Young people need the opportunity to think through the issues at hand. This section will get students talking about the passage of Scripture and interacting on important issues.

reflect

The conclusion to the study will allow students to reflect on some of the issues presented in the study on a more personal level.

meditation

A closing Scripture for the students to read and reflect on.

unit I
extraordinary books

Imagine yourself walking into a party by yourself. You scan a sea of faces, searching for the four friends who said they would meet you there. Finally, you spot Dolores, Chris, Les and Annmarie standing in a circle in the far corner of the room near the food table. Weaving your way through the crowd, you arrive where your friends are standing. Dolores is in the middle of telling a story, but she stops as you greet your friends. Dolores resumes telling her story, which appears to be about two-thirds finished. When she concludes her story, your four friends burst out laughing, but you don't understand what's so funny. Why? You missed the first two-thirds of the story.

Let me ask you this question: How much of the story are you telling your students? There seems to be a nationwide youth ministry trend toward spending most of our time teaching students about the life of Christ, the writings of Paul and the stories of the early Church—all of which are vital to Christian growth, but none of which capture the entire story of Scripture.

You may fear that your students will respond to your attempts to teach about the Old Testament with one word: "Boring." How far from the truth! The Old Testament is bursting with stories of conflict, war, envy, jealousy, miracles and healing. Anyone who views the Old Testament as boring has probably not read it—or maybe they spent all their time in Leviticus and Numbers!

This unit is designed to give your students an overview of four key books in the Old Testament. Each session is designed to give you a flavor of the overall book by analyzing one slice from it. Each session gives you the opportunity to interact with your students, helping them understand the life of the Old Testament.

Thank you, dear friend, for being committed to helping students understand the complete story of Scripture. May you, as well, enjoy learning from its extraordinary adventures.

genesis: creation and curse

He said to me, "My grace is sufficient for you, for my power is made
perfect in weakness." Therefore I will boast all the more gladly
about my weaknesses, so that Christ's power may rest on me.

2 CORINTHIANS 12:9

An unknown Confederate soldier wrote these powerful words:

I asked God for strength that I might achieve.
I was made weak that I might learn humbly to obey.
I asked God for health that I might do great things.
I was given infirmity that I might do better things.
I asked for riches that I might be happy.
I was given poverty that I might be wise.
I asked for power that I might have the praise of men.
I was given weakness that I might feel the need of God.
I asked for all things that I might enjoy life.
I was given life that I might enjoy all things.

I got nothing I asked for
but everything I had hoped for . . .
Almost despite myself, my unspoken
prayers were answered.
I am among all people most richly blessed.

Somehow, this soldier understood the truth of 2 Corinthians 12:9, quoted above, and the truth behind this session. It is not what you have or even how good you are, but rather who you know. God created the world, humankind sinned and Christ redeemed us. Our Christian faith is all about God and relying on His strength, not about using our own strength. The apostle Paul wrote it like this: "The foolishness of God is wiser than man's wisdom, and the weakness of God is stronger than man's strength" (1 Corinthians 1:25).

In your weakest moments, don't be afraid to lean on the strong and steady arms of your Savior. As you introduce your students to this session's description of God's creation, our weakness in sin and the Good News of His redemption, please be reminded that, like the Confederate soldier, God can use us despite our imperfections. Isn't God good?

Bring Him your weakness and find strength in His might.
JACK HAYFORD

genesis: creation and curse

starter

CREATIVE CREATIONS: Get together with four or five people and get creative with the following questions:

1. What's the strangest, most bizarre invention that you've ever heard of?

2. What's the most useful creation or invention you use regularly?

_____

_____

_____

_____

3. If you could create or invent anything, what would it be?

_____

_____

_____

_____

Now, with clay or Play-Doh, make a prototype of your group's best invention idea. It doesn't have to work, but try your best to sculpt a model of the finished product. Now share your small group's answers and brilliant creation with the larger group (and, if time allows, vote on the most promising invention!).

message

Today we're going to take a close look at our human family's origins. Here's something to keep in mind: Sometimes when we read the Bible, we forget that the stories in it are about real people with real feelings, thoughts and motivations. The following questions can help us put ourselves in the "shoes" (metaphorically speaking, of course, since Adam and Eve were naked a good bit of the time) of the characters.

Individually or in a group, read Genesis 2:4–3:19. If you're feeling creative, assign each person in your group a part and act out the drama that took place between Eve, the serpent, Adam and God. Once you've read the passage, answer the following questions on your own or as part of a group discussion.

1. How do you think Adam felt when God told him that he would have a partner?

    _____

    _____

    _____

    _____

    _____

2. Why do you think Eve would want to be like God?

    _____

    _____

    _____

    _____

    _____

3. How do you think the serpent must have felt as Eve bit into the forbidden fruit?

    _____

    _____

    _____

    _____

    _____

4. What might Adam and Eve have been thinking as they were sewing fig leaves together to cover themselves?

5. What would you guess was God's tone of voice when He spoke to Adam and Eve in Genesis 3:11?

6. As Adam was explaining to God that it was all Eve's fault, how do you think Eve felt?

7. If you were Adam, what would you have wanted to say to
    Eve after God explained the curse?

    ....

    ....

    ....

    ....

    ....

    ....

8. What would you have wanted to say to Adam if you were
    Eve?

    ....

    ....

    ....

    ....

    ....

    ....

9. Do you think Adam and Eve were sorry for what they did
    or sorry that they were caught (or both)? Why do you
    think this?

    ....

    ....

    ....

    ....

    ....

    ....

dig

There was a progression in Adam and Eve's feelings about their sin. First they felt good, then they felt ashamed and then they were afraid. Get into pairs to answer the following questions:

1. Think about a temptation you are struggling with in your life right now. How would giving in to it make you feel good, at least at first?

   ....

   ....

   ....

   ....

2. How might giving in to this temptation later make you feel ashamed?

   ....

   ....

   ....

   ....

3. Read 1 John 4:15-18. Adam and Eve went from ashamed of their sin to afraid of God. Why don't we need to be afraid, even when we sin?

   ....

   ....

   ....

   ....

4. Even though we never need to be afraid of God, sin is de-
    structive to our relationship with Him and others—so
    avoid it! Read 1 Corinthians 10:13. How do you think
    God can give you a way out of your temptation this week?

    ....

    ....

    ....

    ....

    ....

    ....

apply

The fallout from Adam and Eve's sin didn't just affect them; we
are still dealing with the consequences today. Ever wonder why
the world is so beautiful and so messed up at the same time?

1. Read Romans 5:12-21. This passage in Paul's letter to the
    Roman church is one of the foundational Scriptures that
    explain the Christian doctrine of *original sin*. Compare
    these verses with Genesis 3:16-19, then do your best to
    come up with a definition for original sin. What does it
    mean that "the result of one trespass was condemnation
    for all men" (Romans 5:18)?

    ....

    ....

    ....

    ....

    ....

    ....

2. Christians have wrestled to pin down a definition of original sin since the Church's earliest days. Most agree that the Fall of humanity resulted in a "sin nature" in all of us, an inability to do the right thing every time. We can't help but "miss the mark," which is what the Greek word *hamart* means—translated into English, "sin." Think about your own struggle to do the right thing every time. How have you "missed the mark"? Do these sins demonstrate the reality of a sin nature? Why or why not?

3. Take another look at Romans 5:12-21. If your sin nature, inherited from Adam and Eve, makes it impossible for you to hit the mark every time on your own, how can you "receive God's abundant provision of grace and of the gift of righteousness" (v. 17)?

4. People aren't the only ones who bear the penalty of the Fall. Read Romans 8:19-22. Do you see humanity's sin nature affecting the natural world? In what ways?

5. Now check out 2 Corinthians 5:17-21. What does it mean to be a "new creation" (v. 17) in light of the curse found in Genesis 3:16-19? What do you think it means for God to have given us the "ministry of reconciliation" (v. 18)?

reflect

There are two different accounts of Creation in the book of Genesis. In chapter 1, God lets us have a look at what He was thinking through the whole process (isn't that amazing?). Read Genesis 1:26-28, and then answer the following questions on your own or with a partner or small group.

1. What do you think it means to be made in God's image?

2. What do you think God had in mind when He said, "Let them rule over the fish of the sea and the birds of the air, over the livestock, over all the earth, and over all the creatures that move along the ground" (v. 26)?

3. How do you think this job, given to humanity by God at the very beginning, relates to Romans 8:19-22, which we read in the previous section?

4. You are created in God's image. On top of that, if you have
    asked Jesus to be your Lord and Savior, you are a new cre-
    ation who is called to be Christ's ambassador of reconcil-
    iation (see 2 Corinthians 5:17-21). Let those facts sink in
    for a minute, and then write a prayer on the lines below
    that expresses your feelings about who you are and what
    you are called to do.

meditation

So God created man in his own image,
in the image of God he created him;
male and female he created them.

GENESIS 1:27

exodus: covenants and commandments

Whoever has my commands and obeys them, he is the one
who loves me. He who loves me will be loved by my Father,
and I too will love him and show myself to him.

JOHN 14:21

The Bible isn't a book of magic formulas for a successful life, but these words are the key principle for living a victorious Christian life. Just as Exodus was written to give the Israelites commandments and covenants from God, these words focus on the same principle: obedience. Basically, Jesus is telling us that the way to show our love for Him is to obey God's commandments—and the result of obedience and love is that He will reveal Himself to us. Love for God equals obedience (our part) and revelation (God's part).

When it comes to loving others, sometimes it isn't easy to follow God's principles. The world says, "Look out for number one!" and "Me first!" The Word, in contrast, says, "Love one another

with a brotherly affection: outdo one another in showing honor"
(Romans 12:10, *RSV*). No one said that living the Christian life
would be easy. The following words from an anonymous writer
can help give us perspective:

IT IS NOT EASY . . .
To apologize.
To begin over.
To take advice.
To be unselfish.
To admit error.
To face a sneer.
To be charitable.
To keep trying.
To be considerate.
To avoid mistakes.
To endure success.
To profit by mistakes.
To forgive and forget.
To think and then act.
To keep out of a rut.
To make the best of little.
To shoulder a deserved blame.
BUT IT ALWAYS PAYS.

Obedience to God is always the best way, but it is most often
not the easiest way. God be with you this session as you present
these incredible truths to students who need to hear them.

The starting point and the goal of our Christian life is obedience.
ANDREW MURRAY

exodus: covenants and commandments

starter

FOLLOW THE RULES . . . OR ELSE: Get together with three or four others and read the following case study. Then discuss the follow-up questions.

> Kelly's father was just laid off from his job, and money is tight around their house. Since Kelly just received her driver's license, she decides to get a job so she can earn some money to help her family.
>
> At her new job at a fast-food restaurant, her boss asks her to sign an "Employee Covenant" in which she agrees to obey the following three rules at the restaurant:

1. She must be on time every day.
2. She must clean the dining area regularly.
3. She must be friendly and courteous to customers.

If she obeys all three rules, she will be promoted and given a raise in salary in one month.

For nearly the whole month, Kelly does a super job being on time, cleaning the restaurant and being friendly. But two days before her first month is up, Kelly gets stuck in traffic and arrives 10 minutes late. Kelly's boss is frustrated. Kelly tries to explain that she got stuck in traffic, but her boss says that she broke the covenant and therefore won't be promoted and receive a raise.

1. Is Kelly's boss being fair? Why or why not?

2. If you were Kelly's boss, what would you do?

message

With the whole group, talk about good rules, bad rules and rules you wish you could change.

1. If you could abolish one rule at your school, what would it be?

    _____

    _____

    _____

    _____

    _____

2. Why is it difficult to obey commands that others give you?

    _____

    _____

    _____

    _____

    _____

3. Name 10 rules that you think are important for parents to teach their children.

    1. _____

    2. _____

    3. _____

    4. _____

5. _____
6. _____
7. _____
8. _____
9. _____
10. _____

Once everybody has their own list, combine everyone's ideas on a whiteboard and then vote for the Top Five Commands for Kids. Then discuss the following:

4. What happens if children do not obey the Top Five Commands for Kids? What are the possible consequences for breaking each rule?

Command 1

Command 2

Command 3

Command 4

Command 5

dig

In the book of Exodus, God clarifies the relationship He wants to have with His people. Read Exodus 19:1-8 to see what type of relationship God wants, then discuss the following questions with a partner or small group.

1. What is a covenant?

   _____

   _____

   _____

   _____

   _____

2. According to verses 5-6, what did God want His people to do?

   _____

   _____

   _____

   _____

3. What did God promise to do in return?

   _____

   _____

   _____

   _____

   _____

4. What does it mean to be "a kingdom of priests and a holy
    nation" (v. 6)?

5. What are the benefits of a covenant relationship with God?

6. How might our covenant relationship with God benefit
    others?

apply

God gave His people the Ten Commandments to give them specific ways to fulfill their part of the covenant. Read Exodus 20:1-17 and then discuss the following questions.

1. Which of the commandments relate to our relationship with God?

2. Which of the commandments relate to our relationship with others?

3. Which commandment do you think is most important?

4. Which commandment do you think is broken most often
   by non-Christians?

5. Which commandment is broken most often by Christians?
   Why do you think this is the case?

6. Which commandment is hardest for you to obey at school?
   Why do have trouble following that rule?

7. Which commandment is hardest for you to obey at home?
    Why is that rule difficult to follow?

_____

_____

_____

_____

_____

_____

_____

reflect

During the Last Supper, the meal that Jesus shared with His dis-
ciples before His trial and execution, Jesus gave His most explicit
commands to those who choose to follow Him. Read John 14:15-
21 and discuss the following questions.

1. In verse 15, what does Jesus say that those who follow
    Him will do? Why will they do this? What does this mean
    to you personally as a follower of Christ?

_____

_____

_____

_____

_____

_____

_____

2. What does Jesus mean in verse 17 when He says that the
    word "cannot accept" the Holy Spirit?

    _____

    _____

    _____

    _____

    _____

    _____

3. In your own words, what does Jesus command in verse 21?
    How do you think His command relates to the Ten Com-
    mandments that God gave in Exodus 20:1-17?

    _____

    _____

    _____

    _____

    _____

    _____

4. Are God's Old Testament covenants and commandments
    still relevant since Jesus came? Why or why not?

    _____

    _____

    _____

    _____

    _____

    _____

    _____

5. The author of the book of Hebrews calls Jesus "the medi-
    ator of a new covenant" (see 9:15). Read Hebrews 8:3-10.
    In verses 5-6, how does the author describe the tabernacle
    in which the priests serve? What does he say about the
    ministry of Jesus?

6. According to verse 9, why was it necessary for God to make
    a new covenant with His people?

7. According to verse 10, what is different about this new
    covenant?

8. How does this relate to Jesus' promise to send the Holy
    Spirit, found in John 14?

    ....

    ....

    ....

    ....

    ....

    ....

9. Write a prayer asking God's Spirit to guide you this week as
    you seek to love Jesus by obeying His commands. Choose a
    prayer partner for the week and pray for each other.

    ....

    ....

    ....

    ....

    ....

    ....

    ....

meditation

Be devoted to one another in brotherly love.
Honor one another above yourselves.

ROMANS 12:10

psalms: problems, prayers and praises

Godliness with contentment is great gain.
For we brought nothing into the world, and we can take nothing out of it.
But if we have food and clothing, we will be content with that.

1 TIMOTHY 6:6-8

Cathy and I had the privilege of staying in a wonderful pastor's home in Romania when I was speaking in that country a few years ago. John and his wife, Elizabeth, lived in a two-room house with their three children. John was the pastor of a 400-member Baptist church and Elizabeth was a nurse working 12-hour shifts, five nights a week. John made $25 a month and Elizabeth brought home $75. John showed me scars he had on his body from being imprisoned for his faith under the evil rule of Ceausescu.

I looked in the children's cardboard toy box and there was an old model car, a doll with a few strands of hair and some old blocks that looked like they had been found in the trash. I thought back to the closets full of toys in our home. The whole time we were getting ready to eat I looked around the house, which, believe me, didn't take a great deal of time. The pastor had four books and his well-worn Bible. The kids slept on a cot and the couch—no beds. The home was what we would call a dump. Their poverty made me feel uncomfortable.

When it was time for dinner, Elizabeth served us, but then didn't eat with us. Cathy thought it was because they didn't have enough food. The meal consisted of a spoonful of sausage and a quarter of a potato. Our water was colored with something red and it had a very foul odor. We drank it, but we just didn't breathe.

As we prepared to eat this terrible-looking sparse meal, our pastor friend grabbed our hands and prayed, "Dear Lord, thank You for our many blessings and thank You for the way You have abundantly provided for us. You are a most gracious and loving God." I sat there stunned and, I must admit, a bit humbled. Here was a man who had been through so much and had so little material goods thanking God for a meal I would have thrown down our garbage disposal. I was reminded that "attitude is everything" and that, as the book of Psalms teaches, even in the midst of trying circumstances there are great reasons to give God praise.

The psalms contain the praises and prayers of the Israelites. It is an honor for us in youth work to introduce such powerful and eternally wonderful words of praise to the next generation.

I complained because I had no shoes until I met a man who had no feet.
INDIAN PROVERB

psalms: problems, prayers and praises

starter

PROBLEM, PRAYER, PRAISE: Get together with a partner or small group and write down a typical teenage problem in two to five sentences. Choose a problem that's broad enough to apply to both girls and guys.

When you're done, exchange papers with another pair or small group so that you have their problem and they have yours. Take a look at their problem and then write a prayer response below it, in two to five sentences. How will you ask God to intervene in the problem?

Finally, exchange that paper with another pair or small group (but not with the ones who received your original). Read the problem and the prayer on the paper you receive and then write a two- to five-sentence praise, responding to the problem and the hope of the prayer.

When all pairs or small groups have finished, share your problem, prayer and praise with the whole group. Then discuss the following questions:

1. Is it sometimes hard to know how to pray about problems in your life? Why or why not?

2. Do you sometimes find it difficult to offer God praise when life is tough? Why or why not?

3. Do you think it's important to praise God even in hard times? Why or why not?

message

The book of Psalms is the songbook of the ancient Israelites. Several different songwriters—including King David—wrote the psalms in various life situations.

Spend even a little time reading the psalms, and you'll notice that they contain at least one of the following: a *problem, prayer* or *praise*. The writers didn't only write happy songs of joyful praise to God, but they also wrote angry songs, sad songs, begging songs and confused songs. When they had a problem, they let God know about it. When they wanted to experience His presence in prayer, they crafted a song to bring their requests. And when they were so overjoyed they could barely stand it, they poured out their praise and sang it to Him at the tops of their lungs.

1. Look up the verses below from the psalms and choose problem, prayer or praise. (Look out! In some cases, the verse may be a combination.)

	Problem	Prayer	Praise
Psalm 130:1-2	☐	☐	☐
Psalm 140:7	☐	☐	☐
Psalm 31:14	☐	☐	☐
Psalm 35:4	☐	☐	☐
Psalm 63:1	☐	☐	☐
Psalm 109:2	☐	☐	☐
Psalm 150:6	☐	☐	☐
Psalm 94:5	☐	☐	☐

Now, with the whole group, read Psalm 120 aloud and discuss the following questions:

2. What is your first "gut reaction" to the tone of this psalm? Do you think it's appropriate for the writer to vent his frustrations to God in this way? Why or why not?

3. When you are hurt or angry, do you feel confident about taking your feelings to God in prayer? Why or why not?

dig

The psalms have a lot to teach us about how to respond to problems in our lives. As we saw in Psalm 120, songwriters like David didn't shy away from expressing their darkest emotions to the Lord. But the psalmists didn't stop there; they asked God to intervene in their troubles in very specific ways.

With the whole group, read Psalm 54:1-7. Notice that this psalm demonstrates a typical pattern in the psalms:

1. Present your *problem* to God.
2. *Pray* that He will intervene.
3. *Praise* Him for what He has already done.

1. Find a partner and break down these verses from Psalm 54 into three parts. State the problem, the prayer and the praise in your own words.

The problem:

_____

_____

_____

_____

The prayer:

_____

_____

_____

_____

The praise:

_____

_____

_____

_____

2. How was David's attitude at the end of the psalm differ-
    ent from his attitude at the beginning?

3. What did David ultimately conclude that God would do
    for Him? What did he state that he would do for God?

4. Now find a different psalm (or portion of a psalm) that
    demonstrates the pattern, and state the problem, the prayer
    and the praise in your own words.

    Psalm:

    The problem:

The prayer:

The praise:

5. How was the writer's attitude at the end of the psalm different from the beginning?

6. From this, what can you see as the benefits of expressing ourselves to God in this way?

apply

1. Now it's time to get personal. With your partner or on
   your own, apply the pattern of the psalms to a problem in
   your own life. State your problem, offer a prayer and then
   give God praise for how you've seen Him at work in the recent past.

   My problem:

   _____

   _____

   _____

   _____

   My prayer:

   _____

   _____

   _____

   My praise:

   _____

   _____

   _____

   _____

2. You can apply the pattern to problems facing your family,
    church, friends, school or city (or even the whole world!).
    State the problem, offer a prayer and then give God praise
    for how you've seen Him at work in this area in the past.

The problem:

_____

_____

_____

_____

_____

_____

My prayer:

_____

_____

_____

_____

_____

_____

My praise:

_____

_____

_____

_____

_____

_____

When you're finished, spend some time with your partner praying for each other's problems and praising God together.

reflect

1. Which psalm is most meaningful to you? Why?

  ....

  ....

  ....

  ....

2. Why do you think many Christians turn to the book of Psalms in times of need?

  ....

  ....

  ....

  ....

  ....

3. Read Psalm 23, a popular passage that is read at many funerals, even of non-Christians. Why do you think the psalms are meaningful even to those who aren't believers?

  ....

  ....

  ....

  ....

If you're ready to dig deeper into a life of prayer and meditation on God's Word, the psalms are a great place to start. During the coming week, read a psalm a day. Read it through slowly once or twice (or even three times), and then try writing your own version. Don't forget the pattern: problem, prayer, praise.

meditation

May the words of my mouth
and the meditation of my heart be pleasing in your sight,
O Lord, my Rock and my Redeemer.

PSALM 19:14

proverbs: choices and consequences

Trust in the LORD with all your heart and lean not on your own understanding;
in all your ways acknowledge him, and he will make your paths straight.
Do not be wise in your own eyes; fear the LORD and shun evil.
This will bring health to your body and nourishment to your bones.

PROVERBS 3:5-8

The book of Proverbs warns us of the positive and negative consequences of making choices. I often like to tell students that many of the decisions they make today will affect them for the rest of their lives. Too often, those of us on the journey of faith do not practice enough wisdom in our lives. The book of Proverbs is loaded with wisdom that, though written thousands of years ago, is still practical for present and future generations.

There is a very old story told about a man in Ireland who was plodding along toward home carrying a huge sack of potatoes.

Finally a friend of his came along with a horse and carriage and offered him a ride. The man gladly accepted the ride, but he kept holding the potatoes over his shoulder. His friend suggested that he lighten his burden by laying the bag in the back of the carriage. In a deep Irish brogue the man replied, "I don't like to trouble you too much, sir. You're a givin' me a ride already, so I'll just carry the potatoes!"

It sounds like such a silly decision by this Irish gentleman, but we often do the same thing when it comes to trusting in God. So often we become weary from the heavy load. Instead of giving our burdens to God, we continue to carry the heavy "bag of potatoes" when the Lord's desire is to carry the burden for us. We experience the negative consequences of our foolish choice to bear the burden alone.

It's true that some burdens are to be borne, but even those become lighter when we choose to give them over to God and lean on Him.

In nature there are neither rewards or punishments—
there are only consequences.
ROBERT GREEN INGERSOLL

proverbs: choices and consequences

starter

MAKE A CHOICE: Each of us makes choices all the time, sometimes without even realizing it, and every choice has consequences (which can be positive, negative or a bit of both). Even when we choose not to choose, we're making a choice!

Think about the choices you've made today—big *and* small— and then consider the consequences. (If you haven't made a big choice today, think about your most recent important decision.)

1. Big choice: _____

_____

_____

The consequences: _____

_____

_____

_____

The consequences if you had made a different choice:

_____

_____

_____

2. Small choice: _____

_____

_____

The consequences: _____

_____

_____

_____

The consequences if you had made a different choice:

_____

_____

_____

3. Do you usually think of the possible consequences of your choices *before* you choose? Why or why not?

_____

_____

_____

_____

message

Let's consider consequences at a deeper level. For each of the following case studies, make your choice: Yes or No. (These are your only options!) Then explain your reasons for making that choice and the possible consequences of your decision.

1. Your friend Krista is dating Greg. You know she really likes him. Another friend, Lisa, tells you that Greg has been flirting with her when Krista is not around. Should you tell Krista what Lisa told you? (Yes or no only!)

   My reasons:

   _____

   _____

   _____

   _____

   _____

   _____

   Possible consequences:

   _____

   _____

   _____

   _____

   _____

   _____

2. You and a bunch of friends are hanging out at Tom's house, waiting for another friend to arrive so you can all go out

together for dinner. As you are waiting, someone suggests that you skip dinner and head for the R-rated movie premiering that night. The rest of the group agrees that it's a good idea, but you've told your parents that you are going to dinner only, and you know they would not approve of this movie. Would you go anyway? (Yes or no only!)

My reasons:

_____

_____

_____

_____

_____

_____

Possible consequences:

_____

_____

_____

_____

3. You notice that your friend Sally is losing a lot of weight. You know that her cheerleading advisor is putting her under a lot of pressure, so you ask her if there's anything wrong. Sally says, "Will you promise not to tell anyone?"

   You answer, "Sure."

   Sally continues, "Well, I think I'm developing an eating disorder. I haven't told anyone yet, not even my parents. You're the first person I've told."

You know Sally's parents and think they would understand and not freak out, but you told Sally you wouldn't tell anyone. Knowing that eating disorders are life-threatening, should you tell Sally's parents? (Yes or no only!)

My reasons:

Possible consequences:

4. Have you ever made a choice that got you into trouble with your parents? If so, what happened?

5. Have you ever made a choice that encouraged a friend or a sibling? If so, what happened?

_____

_____

_____

_____

dig

The book of Proverbs, written mostly by Solomon, King David's son, is full of sayings that warn us of the consequences of our choices. Today we're going to look at the first chapter to see what it teaches about choices and consequences.

Read Proverbs 1:10-19 on your own, with a partner or with the whole group. Answer the questions below and discuss.

1. What choices are described in this passage?

_____

_____

_____

_____

2. What are the consequences of these choices?

_____

_____

_____

_____

3. Now read Proverbs 1:20-32 on your own, with a partner or
    with the group. How are the choices and consequences in
    this passage similar to those in Proverbs 1:10-19?

    ....

    ....

    ....

    ....

    ....

    ....

4. Read Proverbs 1:33. What is the choice made in this verse?

    ....

    ....

    ....

    ....

    ....

    ....

5. How are the consequences in verse 33 different from the
    consequences we have already discussed?

    ....

    ....

    ....

    ....

    ....

    ....

6. The key to all choices is explained in Proverbs 1:7. What does it mean to "fear the LORD"? (*Note*: For a hint, read Proverbs 8:13.)

_____

_____

_____

_____

_____

_____

7. Other parts of Scripture explain that "fearing the Lord" also means acknowledging that there is only one God, who is the Creator and Sustainer of everything, and that we are accountable to Him for every choice we make. When we recognize God's greatness, we love and respect Him so much that we submit to His lordship over our lives by obeying Him. This is "fear" not in the sense of living in terror, but of living in grateful humility that, in His greatness, God loves us. Read 1 Kings 11:1-13 aloud. What distracted Solomon from obedience?

_____

_____

_____

_____

_____

_____

8. How do you think God felt as He described to Solomon the consequences of his choices? What makes you think so?

....

....

....

....

....

apply

Connect with a partner or a small group of three or four other people, and discuss the following questions. When you are finished, spend 5 to 10 minutes in prayer for the choices you each will make in the upcoming week.

1. What is this biggest choice you are facing this week?

....

....

....

....

....

2. What would be a foolish option to choose in this situation?

....

....

....

....

3. What are the possible consequences of a foolish choice?

4. What would be a wise choice to make in this situation?

5. What are the possible consequences?

6. What kind of encouragement or support do you need from others in order to make a wise choice?

reflect

One smart way to approach decision-making is to learn from the mistakes of others. This week, sit down with a parent or another adult you respect and interview him or her about past bad choices. Remember: Listen as you would want to be listened to—without judging! Ask the following questions:

1. What is one of the worst choices you made when you were a teenager?

    ....

    ....

    ....

    ....

    ....

2. Why did you make that choice?

    ....

    ....

    ....

    ....

3. What were the consequences of your choice?

    ....

    ....

    ....

    ....

    ....

4. If you had to do it all over again, how would you change
   your choice?

   ....

   ....

   ....

   ....

   ....

   ....

Once you've heard his or her story, reflect on their choices and
then answer the following questions.

5. What can you learn from the mistakes your parent or
   adult friend made as a teenager?

   ....

   ....

   ....

   ....

   ....

6. How can he or she support you in your efforts to make
   wise choices?

   ....

   ....

   ....

   ....

   ....

   ....

Ask your parent or adult friend to pray with you about the choices you have to make, and let him or her know how you'd like him or her to support you in your efforts. Schedule a regular check-in time to stay on top of your choices.

meditation

The fear of the LORD is the beginning of knowledge,
but fools despise wisdom and discipline.

PROVERBS 1:7

unit II

our extraordinary God

"When I was a teenager, I used to view God as a bank president. He looked 55 years old, sat behind a huge mahogany desk and wore a three-piece suit. I had to come to Him with my requests and needs, just hoping that He would approve them."

This comment from a youth worker friend of mine provoked my thinking. *How do the students who sit in front of me week after week view God?*

As a bank president?

As a Santa Claus, jolly and happy, ready to give good gifts?

As an old, frail grandfather?

As a combination of all three?

If we were to dive into the brains of our students, I think we would be surprised—and scared—at how little they truly know about God.

The images of God in the Old Testament can help wipe the smudges off of the lenses through which we view Him.

He is the Creator.

The Provider.

The Pillar of Cloud by day and Fire by night.

The Miracle Worker.

The great "I Am."

The Holy One.

The Shepherd.

The Father.

This unit has been designed to help you steer your students past the false views they may have of God in order to see how extraordinary He truly is. A fulfilling relationship with God is impossible apart from an understanding of His true nature. Anything less leaves our students (and ourselves!) limping along the path of growth.

Please be in prayer that God will reveal Himself—His extraordinary Self—to your students as you study each of these four sessions together.

a God who keeps His promises

Be strong and courageous. . . . The LORD himself goes before
you and will be with you; he will never leave you nor forsake you.
Do not be afraid; do not be discouraged.

DEUTERONOMY 31:7-8

As the title of this chapter reads, God keeps His promises. A promise is a vow, a declaration or a pledge. Did you know that there are more than three thousand promises in the Bible? God's promises are words that we can trust, and in them we can find great comfort. Over the years, I have created a small list of promises from God that are close to my heart. Often I read them when I am down, tired, drained or simply in need of a wonderful reminder of God's faithfulness. The following are words of strength and promises for you:

promises of His unfailing love:
" 'Though the mountains be shaken and the hills be removed, yet my unfailing love for you will not be shaken nor my covenant of peace be removed,' says the LORD, who has compassion on you" (Isaiah 54:10).

"For God so loved the world that he gave his one and only son, that whoever believes in him shall not perish but have eternal life" (John 3:16).

promises of His forgiveness
"If we confess our sins, he is faithful and just and will forgive us our sins and purify us from all unrighteousness" (1 John 1:9).

"All the prophets testify about him that everyone who believes in him receives forgiveness of sins through his name" (Acts 10:43).

promises of His comfort
"But from everlasting to everlasting the LORD's love is with those who fear him, and his righteousness with their children's children" (Psalm 103:17).

"And surely I am with you always, to the very end of the age" (Matthew 28:20).

promises of His guidance
"But the Counselor, the Holy Spirit, whom the Father will send in my name, will teach you all things and will remind you of everything I have said to you" (John 14:26).

"But when he, the Spirit of truth, comes, he will guide you into all truth. He will not speak on his own; he will speak only what he hears, and he will tell you what is yet to come" (John 16:13).

promises of His joy

"Nehemiah said, 'Go and enjoy choice food and sweet drinks, and send some to those who have nothing pre-pared. This day is sacred to our Lord. Do not grieve, for the joy of the LORD is your strength'" (Nehemiah 8:10).

"Until now you have not asked for anything in my name. Ask and you will receive, and your joy will be complete" (John 16:24).

promises of freedom from guilt

"In him and through faith in him we may approach God with freedom and confidence" (Ephesians 3:12).

"If you, O LORD, kept a record of sins, O LORD, who could stand? But with you there is forgiveness; therefore you are feared" (Psalm 130:3-4).

God don't sponsor no flops!
ETHEL WATERS

a God who keeps His promises

starter

PROMISE KEEPERS: Which of these people do you think would keep a promise?

- ❑ A politician who promises to act in the interest of the voters, not in his or her own interests.
- ❑ A close friend who promises that he (or she) won't tell anyone that you want to break up with your girl-friend (or boyfriend).
- ❑ A parent who promises to leave work early to come to your basketball game.

   ❏   A witness in a court case who promises to tell the whole truth and nothing but the truth.

   ❏   A school teacher who promises that the final exam will be easy.

1. Which of these people do you think would be the *best* promise keeper? Why?

_____

_____

_____

_____

_____

_____

2. Who in your life is best at keeping his or her promises?

_____

_____

_____

_____

_____

_____

message

It was the third quarter of the homecoming football game. Mike, one of the defensive linemen, was sitting on the bench peering anxiously into the crowd. His dad had promised to come to the game—Mike was a senior and this was his dad's last chance to see him in action. Mike knew that his dad had an important business appointment that afternoon, but he had hoped that his dad would keep his promise. Mike hoped in vain. His dad never made it to the game.

1. What is wrong with Mike's dad making a promise that he didn't keep?

_____

_____

_____

_____

_____

2. Who is Mike's dad hurting by breaking this promise? In what way?

_____

_____

_____

_____

3. What would you say to Mike?

_____

_____

_____

_____

_____

4. What would you say to Mike's dad?

    _____

    _____

    _____

    _____

    _____

    _____

5. It has been said that our response to our problems reflects
    our concept of God. Do you agree or disagree with that
    idea? Why?

    _____

    _____

    _____

    _____

    _____

    _____

6. What is one problem that you are dealing with right now?

    _____

    _____

    _____

    _____

    _____

    _____

7. When you think about your problem, how do you feel? Hopeless? Hopeful? Depressed? Joyful? Angry? Peaceful?

    ....

    ....

    ....

    ....

    ....

8. Describe your concept of God. What is He like? What are His character traits?

    ....

    ....

    ....

    ....

    ....

9. Now look at your concept of God (question 8) and your feelings about your problem (question 7) side by side. Do your feelings about your problem reflect your concept of God? Why or why not?

    ....

    ....

    ....

    ....

    ....

dig

Although God has an infinite number of extraordinary qualities, today we are going to study just one of them: *He is a promise-keeping God.* We can see this especially in His faithfulness to His promises to Abraham.

1. Read Genesis 12:1-5. In your own words, what are the promises that God made to Abraham?

   _____

   _____

   _____

   _____

   _____

   _____

2. How did Abraham respond to God's promises and commands?

   _____

   _____

   _____

   _____

   _____

   _____

3. At the heart of God's promises to Abraham was His promise that Abraham would have many descendants and that through those descendants all the families of the earth would be blessed. But Abraham and Sarah had one major

problem: They were getting older and still they had no children. Abraham was 100 years old and Sarah was 90 years old—far from ideal childbearing age (see Genesis 17:15-17)! Read Genesis 18:1-15. What did the Lord promise to Abraham and Sarah? How did Sarah respond?

_____

_____

_____

_____

_____

4. Explain Genesis 18:13-14 in your own words.

_____

_____

_____

_____

_____

5. Read Genesis 21:1-7. If you had been a friend of Abraham and Sarah's, what would you have told them as they proudly showed baby Isaac to you for the first time?

_____

_____

_____

_____

_____

6. What do you think Abraham would say to anyone who doubts that God will keep His promises?

_____

_____

_____

_____

_____

7. Read Romans 4:18-22. Do you think Abraham's response to his problem (supposedly being too old to have kids) reflected his concept of God? Why or why not?

_____

_____

_____

_____

_____

apply

1. In your own words, summarize God's promises to you in each of these passages:

Jeremiah 29:11:

_____

_____

_____

_____

John 3:16:

_____

_____

_____

_____

_____

Philippians 1:6:

_____

_____

_____

_____

Hebrews 13:5:

_____

_____

_____

_____

2. Which promise found in these passages is the most mean-
    ingful to you today? Why?

_____

_____

_____

_____

_____

_____

3. How can you live according to that promise this week?

4. What encouragement can you gain from knowing that God will always keep the promises He has made in Scripture?

5. What prevents you from trusting in God's promises?

6. What can you do to overcome this obstacle?

reflect

1. Do you think God ever delays in fulfilling His promises? Why or why not?

   _____

   _____

   _____

   _____

   _____

   _____

2. When God doesn't seem to be fulfilling His promises in the way we want Him to, what should we do?

   _____

   _____

   _____

   _____

   _____

   _____

3. Why do you think God often fulfills His promises according to His own timetable instead of ours?

   _____

   _____

   _____

   _____

   _____

   _____

4. How can you encourage a friend who is doubting whether
   God will keep His promises?

   _____

   _____

   _____

   _____

   _____

   _____

5. Read Romans 4:23-25. What is God's promise to you in
   this passage?

   _____

   _____

   _____

   _____

   _____

   _____

   _____

6. What does it mean for you that God keeps His promises?
   Do you feel any differently about your problem? Why or
   why not?

   _____

   _____

   _____

   _____

   _____

   _____

7. Write a prayer on the lines below, thanking God for His faithful promise-keeping. If you are having trouble trusting that God will keep His promises, be honest about your doubts and ask God to help you trust Him more deeply.

meditation

Abraham believed the Lord, and he credited it

to him as righteousness.

GENESIS 15:6

a God who works miracles

Again the Jews picked up stones to stone him, but Jesus said to them,
"I have shown you many great miracles from the Father.
For which of these do you stone me? Do not believe me unless I do
what my Father does. But if I do it, even though you do not believe me,
believe the miracles, that you may know and understand that the
Father is in me, and I in the Father."
JOHN 10:31-32,37-38

Do you believe in miracles? I do. I don't believe that everything called a miracle really is a miracle; in fact, I've been disappointed more than once with something or someone who faked a miracle. Yet miracles happen all around us every day. Some of the miracles are extraordinary; others, like a sunset, the human body or the true love of a man and woman, have become so ordinary that we hardly call them a miracle even though that's exactly what they are.

What is a miracle? A miracle is an opening in the wall that separates this world and another. A miracle is a wonder, a beam of God's supernatural power injected into history. A miracle is a happening that cannot be explained in terms of ordinary life.

Christ performed at least 35 miracles according to the Bible. These included walking on water, healing the sick, multiplying loaves and fish, turning water into wine and even raising the dead. Why did Christ perform so many miracles? Did He do it to demonstrate His power to the people or to solidify their faith? Did He do miracles to dramatically show that God took an interest in His creation? The answer is yes. Jesus performed miracles in order to give God glory. Perhaps the greatest miracle was the fact that Jesus—the Word—became flesh and dwelt among us. He is the visible expression of the invisible God.

God doesn't always perform miracles at our every petition, but don't underestimate His power. Next time you seek a miracle, don't forget that He is not a magician—but don't be surprised if His miracle is greater than anything you could ever imagine.

Miracles are a retelling in small letters of the very same story which is written across the whole world in letters too large for some of us to see.

C. S. Lewis

a God who works miracles

starter

BELIEVE IT OR NOT: Stand in the supermarket checkout line and you'll see unbelievable, screaming headlines that announce all kinds of "miracles." Unusual births (67-Year-Old Woman Gives Birth to Two-Headed Cat!), crazy diets (Lose 40 Pounds in One Week!) and visits from extraterrestrials (Aliens in Pittsburgh!) are pretty standard front-page tabloid fare.

The reason why some people are taken in by these outrageous claims is that *miracles do happen.* Of course, the vast majority of "news" reported in tabloids is a crackpot collection of doctored photos and pseudo-science. Plus, not everything that's inexplicable is a miracle. But that doesn't mean that miracles don't happen.

Note: You can download this group study guide in 8$\frac{1}{2}$" x 11" format at **www.gospellight.com/uncommon/the_old_testament.zip.**

Get together with a group of four or five other students. On a large piece of poster board or newsprint, create your own version of a tabloid front page—only this time, the miracles will be real! Grab your Bible and some markers or colored pencils, and start with the headline "You Won't Believe What God Did!"

The job of your editorial team is to hunt down some good miracles found in the Old Testament and design a front page that announces God's unbelievable works. Choose three or four Old Testament miracles and then write some catchy headlines and draw pictures that will show your reading audience what they will find when they crack open God's Word.

When you're done, share your "front page" with the whole group!

message

Now huddle with your small group and answer the following questions.

1. List at least two miraculous answers to prayer that are found in the Old Testament.

   Miracle 1: _____

   Who prayed, and what did he or she pray for?

   _____

   _____

   _____

   _____

   _____

What happened as a result?

_____

_____

_____

_____

_____

_____

_____

Miracle 2: _____

Who prayed, and what did he or she pray for?

_____

_____

_____

_____

_____

_____

What happened as a result?

_____

_____

_____

_____

_____

_____

_____

2. Now List at least two miraculous answers to prayer from your own life.

Miracle 1: _____

What did you pray for?

_____

_____

_____

_____

_____

What happened as a result?

_____

_____

_____

_____

_____

_____

Miracle 2: _____

What did you pray for?

_____

_____

_____

_____

What happened as a result?

_____

_____

_____

_____

_____

_____

_____

3. Which list—Old Testament miracles or miracles in your life—was easier to come up with? Why?

_____

_____

_____

_____

_____

_____

_____

4. Do you think God worked more miracles in the past than He does in the present? Why or why not?

_____

_____

_____

_____

_____

_____

_____

5. Some Christians claim that God works just as many miracles today as in the past, but that we don't always notice them. Do you think that's true? Why or why not?

_____

_____

_____

_____

_____

_____

dig

There are a ton of miracles recorded in the Old Testament. One particular prophet, Elijah, experienced three major miracles . . . all in one day! With a partner or small group, be a "journalist" to investigate what happened.

miracle #1: the ruin of baal

1. Read 1 Kings 18:16-40. At the beginning of the passage, what was Israel's attitude toward God?

_____

_____

_____

_____

_____

2. How do you think the 450 prophets of Baal and 400 prophets of Asherah felt as they saw lone Elijah, the prophet of God, walking up Mount Carmel?

3. In your own words, how would you describe what happened in verses 25-29?

4. Using three words, describe Elijah's attitude in verses 36 and 37.

5. Why did Elijah order the prophets of Baal to be killed?

_____

_____

_____

_____

_____

_____

miracle #2: the rain

1. Read 1 Kings 17:1 and 1 Kings 18:41-45. Why did God choose that particular day to bring rain to the dry land?

_____

_____

_____

_____

_____

_____

_____

2. What does this passage tell you about Elijah's faith in God?

_____

_____

_____

_____

_____

_____

miracle #3: the run

1. Read 1 Kings 18:45-46. What do you suppose Ahab was thinking as Elijah raced ahead of him, even though Ahab was riding a horse-drawn chariot?

_____

_____

_____

_____

_____

_____

_____

2. What do these two verses tell us about God's power that is within us?

_____

_____

_____

_____

_____

_____

_____

apply

The Old Testament is exploding with examples of God's miracles. Often these miracles followed persistent prayer on the part of His people. Read 1 Kings 17:17-24 out loud, with a partner or small group, and then discuss the following questions.

1. Why do you think God did the miracle of healing the woman's son?

2. How did the woman respond to God's miracle?

3. The same God is working today, and He wants to work miracles in our lives. Our part is to seek Him through prayer. What miracle would you like to see God do in your life?

4. What miracle would you like God to work in your family?

    ....

    ....

    ....

    ....

    ....

    ....

5. What miracle would you like to see God work in your youth group or church community?

    ....

    ....

    ....

    ....

    ....

    ....

6. What miracle would you like to see God work in your neighborhood or city?

    ....

    ....

    ....

    ....

    ....

    ....

reflect

Often, our prayers to God are requests that others could help us with. We ask for help taking a test, healing for a sore ankle or just to have a good day. There's nothing wrong with involving God in every aspect of our lives, no matter how small—and He often does answer prayer by sending friends or experts who can help us solve a problem, heal a wound or feel better. However, God is a big God. He wants to work in big ways. Join up with a prayer partner and discuss the following questions. Then spend 5 to 10 minutes in prayer, focusing on the "big things" each of you is asking for from God.

1. If God can heal any sickness, why doesn't He heal every sickness?

    ....

    ....

    ....

    ....

    ....

2. What do you do when you believe God for a miracle, but nothing seems to happen?

    ....

    ....

    ....

    ....

    ....

3. Is every act of God a miracle? Why or why not?

4. What's a big request you want to ask of God?

5. What, if anything, is keeping you from asking God to move in a miraculous way?

Take a few minutes to pray for "big things" for one another. Be as specific as you can in your prayer, and then wait for the next few days, weeks or months to see how God answers!

meditation

You are the God who performs miracles;
you display your power among the peoples.

PSALM 77:14

a God who opposes sin

But God demonstrates his own love for us in this:
While we were still sinners, Christ died for us.

ROMANS 5:8

There is a scene from the movie *Chariots of Fire* that is forever embedded in my mind. The film tells the true story of Eric Liddell, who went to the 1924 Olympics in Paris, France. He was assigned to run the 100-yard dash on Sunday. But there was one thing this incredible athlete took more seriously than his running, and that was his faith.

For Liddell, his faith told him that he could not run on Sunday. All efforts to persuade him otherwise failed. A British dignitary finally cried out in frustration, "What a pity we couldn't have persuaded him to run."

After a moment's pause, Liddell's coach responded, "It would have been a pity if we had, because we would have separated him from the source of his speed."

Eric Liddell's obedience to God was his source of strength and purpose. And his firm stand for God helped him to be one of the most inspiring athletes of the twentieth century.

God doesn't oppose sin because He is the great killjoy, but rather because He knows that sin keeps us from our source of power to live the life of purpose, strength and joy He created us to live.

How about you? Is your desire to serve Jesus greater than any of your other desires? This session is a good time to take another look at your own priorities. I've never met a person who put God first in his or her life and ever regretted it.

I don't know what the future holds, but I know who holds the future.

E. STANLEY JONES

a God who opposes sin

starter

HATE IT: Get together with a group of two other people and see how much you have in common. In three minutes or less, list things (not people!) that all three of you hate (for example, broccoli or homework). Go!

Now that you've got your list of everything the three of you hate,
it's time to think about what God hates. List everything you can
think of in three minutes or less. Bonus if you can find Scripture
verses to support your items!

_____

_____

_____

_____

_____

_____

Share your lists with the larger group and then discuss the following questions:

1. What are the three most common things everybody hates?

    _____

    _____

    _____

    _____

    _____

2. What are the three things that pretty much everyone agrees
    that God hates?

    _____

    _____

    _____

    _____

    _____

3. Where in the Bible does it say God hates these things?

_____

_____

_____

_____

_____

_____

_____

message

Now get together with a partner and come up with a scenario in which a high school student does something wrong. We're talking about *on-purpose trouble,* the kind that happens when you know what you should do and choose not to do it, or know what you *shouldn't* do and choose to do it anyway (a good example is cheating on a test). Once you're done, combine with another set of partners and discuss your scenario and theirs. Then answer the following questions together.

1. Who is affected by the teen's actions?

_____

_____

_____

_____

_____

_____

_____

2. By whose standards is the student's behavior wrong?

3. What consequences should he or she suffer?

4. Who should be responsible for delivering the consequences?

5. Why should the teen have chosen to do right instead of wrong?

dig

God loves us more than we can possibly imagine—and that is why He hates it when we sin. Choosing to sin—to reject what we know is right and do what is wrong—breaks down our relationships with God and with each other. When we truly love someone, we do everything in our power to do the right thing for him or her—and sinning is exactly the opposite of that deep level of commitment.

One of the words for "sin" in the New Testament is *hamartia*, which can be translated "missing the mark." This is a powerful picture to help us understand how damaging sin can be: When we choose to do wrong, we miss out on everything that is most important—communion with God and friendship with others.

With the whole group, read Joshua 7:1-26, which recounts a time when all of Israel, God's people, suffered because of sin. Then discuss the following questions.

1. Why did God's anger burn, according to Joshua 7:1?

2. Why did Joshua and the Israelites lose the battle at Ai, according to verses 2-12?

3. According to verses 13-18, why was it important for the Is-
    raelites to consecrate themselves? (If you need to, look up
    the word "consecrate" in a dictionary.)

    _____

    _____

    _____

    _____

    _____

    _____

    _____

4. Why did Achan take some of the riches from Ai, according
    to verses 19-24?

    _____

    _____

    _____

    _____

    _____

    _____

5. Why do you think God would want Achan to be killed?

    _____

    _____

    _____

    _____

    _____

    _____

6. Why did the Israelites also kill Achan's children and his animals?

7. Why do you think God allowed all of Israel to suffer for one person's sin?

8. How do you think this story demonstrates the truth that sin destroys relationships between God and others?

apply

Find a partner with whom to discuss the following questions. Choose someone with whom you feel comfortable talking honestly, and keep in mind that each other's answers should be confidential between the two of you.

1. Do you think that teenagers, in general, hate sin? Why or why not?

   _____

   _____

   _____

   _____

   _____

   _____

2. What is one common sin that teens commit?

   _____

   _____

   _____

   _____

3. Why do you think this sin is so common?

   _____

   _____

   _____

   _____

   _____

4. What do you think are some of the factors that lead a person into sin?

5. Do you think God always withdraws His blessing from our lives when we sin (as He did with Israel because of Achan's sin)? Why or why not?

6. You've probably heard the phrase "God hates the sin but loves the sinner." What does this mean to you?

7   In what areas are you personally missing the mark?

8. How do you see your sin standing in the way of your relationship with God?

9. How do you see your sin standing in the way of your relationships with others?

10. How can your partner help you hit the mark in the coming week?

_____

_____

_____

_____

_____

reflect

The Bible teaches in Romans 3:23 that "all have sinned and fall short of the glory of God." Read Proverbs 6:16-19 and reflect on the following questions.

1. In today's language, how would you rewrite the seven sins found in these verses?

_____

_____

_____

_____

2. Based on experiences from your own life, what are some examples of the seven sins?

_____

_____

_____

_____

_____

3. Which of the seven sins do you most often fall into? Why?

4. Why do you think that these seven sins are so detestable to God?

5. The word "grace" is sometimes defined as "God's unmerited favor." In other words, when God shows us grace, He acts kindly toward us even though we don't deserve it. Can you recall a time when God showed you grace, even when you knew He was opposed to your sin? What happened?

6. Take a few minutes to write a prayer of thankfulness for
    God's love for and kindness toward you. If there is an area
    of your life in which you are missing the mark, ask His for-
    giveness and pray for the Holy Spirit's power and wisdom
    as you try to hit the mark instead.

_____

_____

_____

_____

_____

_____

_____

meditation

But God demonstrates his own love for us in this:
While we were still sinners, Christ died for us.

Romans 5:8

a God who forgives

*If we confess our sins, he is faithful and just and will forgive us
our sins and purify us from all unrighteousness.*

1 JOHN 1:9

At a conference for United States governors several years ago, an interesting question was raised during one of the political debates: "What is the greatest thing in the world?" It was absolutely quiet. None of the governors had an answer. Finally a young aide took the microphone and said, "The greatest thing in the world is that we can walk away from yesterday."

I'm not even sure if that young aide knew that she had just summarized the essence of the gospel of Jesus Christ. The good news of the Christian faith is that we can walk away from yesterday. The apostle Paul could walk away from his persecution of the Christians and answer the call to Christ (see Acts 9:1-19). The woman taken in adultery could walk away from her destructive lifestyle into a new life with Jesus (see John 8:2-11). Matthew could walk away from his job as a crooked tax collector and follow Jesus into a new life (see Mark 2:13-14). The prodigal son could walk away from his life of moral failure in the far country and walk into the loving, forgiving arms of his father (see Luke 15:11-32).

To be able to walk away from the failures and guilt of yesterday lies at the very heart of forgiveness. This is no call to cop out, drop out or otherwise escape responsibility, but it is a liberating message that no one—absolutely no one—is tied to a past from which there is no release. The gospel gladly sings of the possibility of new beginnings. Aren't you glad you are a Christian?

When it comes to confessed sins, our Lord is absent-minded.

PETER GILCHRIST

a God who forgives

starter

FROM A TO Z: Get together with a group of three or four friends and make an "Alphabet Praise List." This is the way it's done: For every letter of the alphabet, name one characteristic of God. (For example: *Awesome*, *Beautiful*, *Compassionate*, and so forth. But think of your own words!) When you're done, share your list with the whole group.

A: _____

B: _____

C: _____

D: _____

E: _____

F: _____

G: ....

H: ....

I: ....

J: ....

K: ....

L: ....

M: ....

N: ....

O: ....

P: ....

Q: ....

R: ....

S: ....

T: ....

U: ....

V: ....

W: ....

X: ....

Y: ....

Z: ....

message

With a partner or small group, read the stories below and answer the questions.

Volleyball tryouts are quickly approaching, so you and your friend decide to practice volleyball after school at your house. It's so hot outside that you decide to practice inside your living room. There's plenty of room and it's air-conditioned.

Your little sister warns you, "You're not supposed to play ball in the house."

"No big deal," you reply, "we'll be careful."

Just as you finish this sentence, there's a loud CRASH! Peering down at the floor, you see the shattered remnants of what had once been an expensive mirror near your front door. Your friend spiked the ball, and you weren't there to block.

A few seconds later, your mom runs into the room and asks, "What happened? How did the mirror get broken?" You've been caught!

1. How do you respond?

   ☐ Ask innocently, "What mirror?"
   ☐ Argue, "I never liked that mirror anyway."
   ☐ Tell her that your friend did it.
   ☐ Admit what happened, but be defensive about it.
   ☐ Admit what happened and ask for forgiveness.
   ☐ Admit what happened, ask for forgiveness and offer to pay for a new mirror.

2. Why is our first reaction so often to blame others for our mistakes?

   _____

   _____

   _____

   _____

   _____

   _____

3. Why do we hate to get caught?

    _____

    _____

    _____

    _____

4. One day, the well-known author and creator of detective Sherlock Holmes, Sir Arthur Conan Doyle, decided to play a practical joke on his 10 closest friends. He sent each of them a telegram with the following message: *The truth is out. Flee immediately.* All 10 did just that! They left town! Doyle hadn't guessed that his friends were so ashamed of something they had done. Read Romans 3:23. How does this verse relate to this story?

    _____

    _____

    _____

    _____

    _____

5. Do you agree or disagree that most people would flee if they received such a message? Why or why not?

    _____

    _____

    _____

    _____

6. What should a person who feels guilty do?

---

dig

David, a leader anointed by God to be king over His people, experienced many personal and spiritual triumphs. However, he was human. He made mistakes. He committed sins. One particular sin of David's is recorded in 2 Samuel 11–12. Team up with one or two study buddies and find out what happened.

the bad news

1. Read 2 Samuel 11:1-17. At what point did David's sin begin?

---

2. Who else besides David committed sin?

---

3. What do we learn from these verses about Uriah the Hittite?

4. How do you think David was feeling after Uriah refused to sleep with his wife?

5. What was David's state of mind in 2 Samuel 11:14-17?

the good news

1. To see how God got David's attention about his sin, read 2 Samuel 12:1-10. What was Nathan's clever way of convincing David of his sin?

2. God used Nathan to get David's attention. What are some other ways God could have used to get David's attention?

3. Read 2 Samuel 12:13-23. What were the consequences David still had to face, even though he had repented?

4. Why do you think God didn't simply heal David and Bathsheba's son?

5. Why did David's attitude change once his son was dead?

apply

1. Are there any people whom God won't forgive? Explain your answer.

2. Are there any sins God won't forgive? Why or why not?

3. Does God also forget our sins when He forgives us? Explain your answer.

_____

_____

_____

_____

_____

_____

4. For what do you need to ask forgiveness from God right now?

_____

_____

_____

_____

_____

5. Are there any consequences you may still have to face for what you have done? If so, what?

_____

_____

_____

_____

_____

_____

6. What steps do you need to take to make it right?

7. How can you show forgiveness to others this week?

reflect

After David committed adultery with Bathsheba, he asked God for forgiveness. God granted him forgiveness and continued to use David in mighty ways. David's story shows us the power of forgiveness to bring freedom and joy back into our lives. Get together with a prayer partner and discuss the following questions.

1. How have you sinned against a family member recently?

2. Have you asked for forgiveness from that person yet? Why
    or why not?

    _____

    _____

    _____

    _____

    _____

    _____

    _____

3. How would your family be different if you repeatedly con-
    fessed to and forgave each other?

    _____

    _____

    _____

    _____

    _____

    _____

4. How can your family practice forgiving each other in the
    future?

    _____

    _____

    _____

    _____

    _____

    _____

    _____

5. Write a prayer asking God to give you courage and strength to ask for and offer forgiveness in your family. Pray for your prayer partner, too.

meditation

If we confess our sins, he is faithful and just and will forgive us our sins and purify us from all unrighteousness.

1 JOHN 1:9

unit III

ordinary people with extraordinary qualities

Maybe you wanted to be a superhero when you were growing up. Maybe you wanted to have titanium claws like Wolverine from the X-Men or be able to control the weather like Storm. Perhaps you wished you were like Batman with his incredible gadgets or like Susan from the Fantastic 4 with her powers to turn invisible. Heroes like these are appealing because they defend the defenseless and fight for truth, justice and the American way.

Unfortunately, finding a hero these days is not so easy. Students feel distant from their teachers and school administrators, abandoned by their parents and disillusioned by popular athletes and entertainers. So maybe it's time to look in a new direction for our heroes. Maybe it's time that we as youth workers point students to the pages of the Old Testament and the men and women in those pages whose lives were open to doing great things for God.

The cool thing about the heroes of the Old Testament is that they are regular people. As I read about them, I have yet to discover any individual who had superhuman powers on his or her own, or who was always perfect, or who acted like a super saint all of the time. Instead, I see sinners in relationship with God the Father. I see normal, ordinary people with some extraordinary qualities. This is true heroism: Taking what God has given you and doing your best to glorify Him with it.

As your students study this unit, hopefully they will also realize that they too can be ordinary people with extraordinary qualities. They too can try their best to love their Lord with all their heart, mind and soul, and to make His love known to others. May these heroes from the past inspire your students to become godly heroes in the present and future.

samuel: living with your ears open

Who shall separate us from the love of Christ? Shall trouble or
hardship or persecution or famine or nakedness or danger or sword?
As it is written: "For your sake we face death all day long; we are
considered as sheep to be slaughtered." No, in all these things we are
more than conquerors through him who loved us.

ROMANS 8:35-37

For a Christian youth speaker, it had been one of those crummy days. I walked down from the platform of the high school auditorium, feeling depressed and dejected. I hadn't connected with the audience. Basically, what I thought would work at the assembly had fallen flat. I mumbled an apology to the principal and walked to my car, feeling broken and downcast. The entire day, I let this bomb of an assembly get to me.

That night my sleep was interrupted by a dream—I believe God gave me this dream. I found myself in the same auditorium as I was earlier in the day. It was empty except for one person sitting in the front row—Jesus. As I walked to the platform, Jesus rose to His feet and gave me a standing ovation! He cheered, He whistled, He applauded with enthusiasm before I even spoke.

When I awoke, I remember smiling so big, my face hurt. God loves me not for what I do but for who I am: His child.

What about you? Do you know that Jesus daily gives you a standing ovation? He loved you enough to die for you. I have this feeling that if He carries a wallet in heaven, your picture and mine are in there. Isn't it nice to be loved?

Listening is the language of love.
NED BRINES

samuel: living with your ears open

starter

LISTEN UP: With the whole group, spread out around the room as far away as possible from everyone else and then close your eyes. As your youth leader travels around the room, he or she will tap a student on the shoulder. If and when you are tapped, say "Who's talking now?" Feel free to disguise your voice however you want—the point is to make it hard for others to guess who's talking!

When you hear another student say "Who's talking now?" keep your eyes closed and make your best guess. Your youth leader will tap 7 to 10 students during the game, so listen up!

Note: You can download this group study guide in 8¹/₂" x 11" format at **www.gospellight.com/uncommon/the_old_testament.zip.**

When the game is over, discuss the following questions with your group:

1. How were you able to tell who was talking?

2. Which voices were easiest to recognize? Why?

3. Which voices were hardest to recognize? Why?

4. Think of a time when you were talking with someone and it was obvious that they weren't listening to you. How did you feel?

_____

_____

_____

_____

_____

_____

5. Do you ever feel like God isn't listening to you? If so, how does it feel?

_____

_____

_____

_____

_____

6. Do you think God ever feels like *you're* not listening to *Him*? If so, how do you think God feels about it?

_____

_____

_____

_____

_____

_____

message

Team up with a study buddy or small group and get to know some people who learned about listening to God. As you read, notice that Eli, the priest of Shiloh, had difficulties hearing God's voice while Samuel, a young teenager, was available to hear from God.

eli

1. Read 1 Samuel 2:29. What sins did the Lord see in Eli?

2. What were Eli's priorities?

3. How did Eli's wrong priorities muffle his ability to listen for the Lord's voice?

samuel

1. Now let's look at how Samuel shows two important qualities in a person who is able to listen to the Lord: *a desire to
   be close to God* and *a desire to serve God*. Read 1 Samuel 3:1-
   20. Where did Samuel sleep?

   _____

   _____

   _____

   _____

   _____

   _____

2. How does the place where Samuel slept reflect his desire
   to be close to God?

   _____

   _____

   _____

   _____

   _____

3. Can someone who is far from God hear His voice? Why or
   why not?

   _____

   _____

   _____

   _____

   _____

   _____

4. How is Samuel's response to Eli in 1 Samuel 3:5-6,8 similar to his response to God in 1 Samuel 8:10?

5. Why did Samuel refer to himself as God's "servant"?

6. How is a servant attitude important in listening to God's voice?

dig

1. Why do you think Samuel didn't want to tell Eli what God had revealed to Him?

2. Why do you think Eli responded the way he did in 1 Samuel 3:18?

3. In what situations do you think it would be the toughest to share with others what you feel God is leading you to do?

4. Martin Luther, one of the primary leaders of the Reformation, once taught that "prayer changes from talking into being silent. And then our being silent can change into listening to God." This is similar to the words of Jeremiah 33:3: "Call to me and I will answer you and tell you great and mighty things you did not know." What does this passage tell you about the balance between talking and listening to God?

5. What benefits do we receive when we listen to God?

....

....

....

....

....

....

....

....

apply

Get into a small group of three to four and read the following stories, then answer the questions.

A 20-year-old named Loren Cunningham was part of a gospel singing quartet that was traveling to the Bahamas. One night after ministering, Loren laid down on his bed and opened his Bible, asking God to speak into his mind.

Suddenly, he envisioned a map of the world. Only the map was alive, moving! He could see all the continents, with waves from the ocean crashing onto their shores.

The ocean waves became waves of young people—teenagers—covering the continents. They were preaching from house to house. They were praying with strangers. They were caring for people on street corners and outside bars.

Loren wondered, "Was that really You, Lord?"

Loren prayed, "God, is this vision from You? Is my future somehow linked to waves of young people?" God seemed to confirm that it was His vision.

Young people going out as missionaries—what an amazing vision! Based on what the Lord revealed to him, Loren founded an organization known as YWAM—Youth With A Mission. It has been more than 40 years since he had that vision, and hundreds of thousands of young "YWAMers" have swept into every continent to share the gospel.

1. Would you conclude that Loren heard from God?

_____

_____

_____

_____

_____

2. What kind of a person do you think Loren was?

_____

_____

_____

_____

_____

3. Have you ever felt as if you heard from the Lord? If so, what happened?

_____

_____

_____

_____

_____

4. How do we hear God?

5. Danielle, a high school sophomore, had been going to the same church with her parents for 10 years. However, she had only gotten serious about her relationship with Christ a few months ago. Last night at dinner, Danielle's parents told her that, due to the major fights they had been having lately, they felt that God wanted them to file for divorce. Do you think Danielle's parents truly heard God's voice? Explain your answer.

6. God's voice in the present will never contradict His voice in the past, namely Scripture. Besides checking what we think God is saying to us in His Word, how else can we confirm whether what we are hearing is actually God's voice?

7. If you wanted confirmation that you're hearing God's voice from two or three other Christians whom you respect, who would you go to?

....

....

....

....

reflect

Too often, we act as if we are the architects of our own lives. We design our own plans, and sometimes ask God to bless what we have already designed. How far this is from the truth! God is the Master Architect. Our job is to follow His plans, not try to create our own.

1. What are the problems with designing your own blueprint?

....

....

....

....

2. What keeps you from letting God, the Master Architect, give you His blueprint for your life?

....

....

....

....

3. How can you get this week's blueprint from the Master Architect?

_____

_____

_____

_____

_____

4. On your own, spend some time in prayer. Spend the first couple of minutes writing about a specific situation in your life in which you need God's direction. Then put your pen or pencil down and listen. After several minutes of listening for God's voice, write down what you believe His Spirit is saying to you. If you're not sure that it's God you're hearing, seek out a parent, youth leader or pastor who can give you wise guidance.

_____

_____

_____

_____

_____

meditation

Come, my children, listen to me;
I will teach you the fear of the Lord.

PSALM 34:11

esther:
for such a time
as this

And the things you have heard me say in the presence of many witnesses
entrust to reliable [people] who will also be qualified to teach others.
2 TIMOTHY 2:2

A judge in a juvenile court was battling a massive crime wave. Kid after kid was hauled before him, mainly from the same neighborhood. Finally the judge, totally exasperated, questioned the next defendant: "Where did you learn this stuff?" The adolescent replied, "Rocko taught me." When the next case came up, the judge repeated the question: "Who taught you to steal?" The answer was the same: "Rocko did."

Over the next week the judge found 33 juvenile delinquents who had picked up their criminal skills from this now-notorious

Rocko character. Realizing that Rocko was quite possibly the person who was key to cutting the crime rate in this neighborhood, the judge instructed the district attorney to bring Rocko to him.

Two days later Rocko stood before the bench. "Well, what do you have to say for yourself?" the judge demanded. "I've got a jail full of minors whose lives you've corrupted. How could you do such a thing?"

"Eddie taught me," the young man replied.

There's a lesson here for those of us who work with kids. Ordinary people can influence others—for good or for bad. God uses ordinary people to influence young people through personal relationships. God uses any circumstance or relationship to get a person's attention.

Imagine the movement that began with a handful of weak-kneed people in an upstairs room in Jerusalem. By the end of the first century, this small group had turned the world upside down. And today you and I are a part of that same movement! Who knows . . . one day another Christian prophetic voice will lead the Church and someone will ask, "Where did you get your start?"

The reply will be, "My youth worker taught me."

You are the only Jesus somebody knows.
A MISSIONARY FROM AFRICA

esther:
for such a time
as this

starter

IF I WERE . . . If you had one of the jobs below, how could you help others know about God?

An artist
An Olympic athlete
An attorney
A fast-food worker
A state senator
A designer
A teacher
A parent

Note: You can download this group study guide in 8½" x 11" format at **www.gospellight.com/uncommon/the_old_testament.zip.**

Now get together with three or four friends and discuss the following questions.

1. If you could have any job you wanted, what would it be?

2. What would be the best part of the job?

3. How could you help others know about the Lord through this job?

4. Many people believe any job can turn into full-time ministry as God uses a person to reach out to others. The key

is not the job itself, but the person's attitude. Do you agree? Why or why not?

_____

_____

_____

_____

_____

message

Now it's time to get dramatic. The good news is, you don't have to memorize any lines; the Narrator will read everyone's parts while you act it out. Decide who will be each character listed below to put on a melodrama for the whole group. Everyone else will supply the sound effects and "crowd noise." Don't forget to ham it up!

cast

Narrator	Esther (ES-ter)
King Xerxes (ZERK-seez)	Bigthana (Big-THAH-nuh)
Vashti (VASH-tee)	Teresh (TEAR-esh)
Three messengers	Haman (HAY-mun)
Mordecai (MORE-duh-kai)	A guard

There once was a king of Persia named Xerxes. Xerxes was a proud and noble king. One day, he was having a wild party (*sounds of a wild party*). Wanting to impress his friends, he called for his beautiful wife Vashti, "Vashti, come here darling." Vashti was insulted. She sighed loudly and refused to come.

Xerxes was hopping mad (yes, he actually began to hop). He said angrily, "Vashti, I will not think of you as my wife anymore. I need a new wife."

The king sent out messengers to bring many beautiful women to the palace. When Mordecai heard that Xerxes wanted a new wife, he knew that his cousin Esther was lovely and told her, "Esther, skip along to the palace." Sure enough, the king took one look at Esther and fell head over heels in love (yes, he actually did somersaults). He asked her to marry him and she became his queen.

One problem: Mordecai had warned Esther not to tell King Xerxes that she was a Jew. A little while later, two of the king's officers, Bigthana and Teresh, crouched nearby and dreamed up ways to kill Xerxes. Mordecai overheard their plans. He said, "Hark, I must tell Queen Esther to warn the king." Which he did. And then Queen Esther told the king, and the two officers were arrested and hung.

Sometime later the king elevated the evil Haman to a high position and commanded that everyone was supposed to bow low when Haman walked by. However, Mordecai refused to bow down because a Jew only bows down to God. Haman got angry and stomped about. And he kept on stomping until finally he got an idea: "I know," he said. "I'll trick the king into issuing an edict to kill all of the Jews, including Mordecai."

When Mordecai found out that the king had decided to kill all of the Jews, he tore his clothes and wept, moaned and wailed. And all the other Jews did, too (*sounds of moaning, weeping, wailing*). After doing this for a while, he explained the situation to Esther. At first she was frightened, but finally she said, "I've got to put a stop to this."

Interestingly enough, the king had a hard time sleeping one night. He was tossing and turning and suddenly woke up. He grabbed for the nearest book, which happened to be a history of his reign. He read the story about Mordecai saving his life and wondered aloud, "Hmmm . . . I wonder if I ever honored him."

He called, "Haman!" Haman ran into the room. King Xerxes asked, "What should be done for the man the king delights to honor?"

Haman thought the king was talking about him, so he made up an elaborate plan to honor himself. The king liked Haman's plan and exclaimed, "Good! I want you to see that Mordecai is honored in this way." So Haman was forced to give Mordecai honor. Now he was *really* mad at Mordecai and planned to hang him.

Meanwhile, Esther planned a banquet for the king and she also invited Haman. The king, Haman and Esther were all sitting around a table, eating and drinking. Suddenly, the king asked, "What is your petition, Esther?"

Esther asked the king boldly, "Please save my people from death."

The king raged, "Who is this evil man who dares to kill my queen and her people?"

Haman cringed and tried to sneak away. But Esther pointed to the fleeing Haman and declared, "It is Haman who plans this evil deed!"

The king listened carefully to Esther. He had the guard arrest Haman and he had him hung on the very gallows that Haman had built for Mordecai. Esther, Mordecai and all the Jews jumped for joy and yelled, "The Jews have been saved!"

dig

Well done! Now, with the whole group, discuss the following questions.

1. How do you think God worked through Xerxes' seemingly unfair dismissal of Queen Vashti, his first wife?

2. Read Esther 5:9-14. How would you describe Haman?

3. If you were king, would you want Haman as your close advisor? Why or why not?

4. Read Esther 4:11,15-16. How was Esther treated as the
    queen?

    _____

    _____

    _____

    _____

    _____

    _____

5. How could her situation change if the king was displeased
    with her request to save the Jews?

    _____

    _____

    _____

    _____

    _____

    _____

6. How do you think Esther felt when Moredecai insisted
    that she conceal her Jewish identity?

    _____

    _____

    _____

    _____

    _____

    _____

7. What did Mordecai mean in Esther 4:14 when he warned
    Esther, "For if you remain silent at this time, relief and de-
    liverance for the Jews will arise from another place, but
    you and your father's family will perish. And who knows
    but that you have come to royal position *for such a time as
    this?*" (Italics added for emphasis.)

    _____

    _____

    _____

    _____

    _____

    _____

    _____

8. In your own words, what was Esther's reply to Mordecai?

    _____

    _____

    _____

    _____

    _____

    _____

    _____

apply

Now find a partner and discuss the following questions. Choose
someone with whom you can be honest!

1. What prevents us from obeying God when He calls us to do certain things at certain times?

2. What might be some of the consequences for others if we refuse to obey God?

3. What might be some of the consequences in our own lives if we refuse to obey God's call?

4. How is God calling you to act "for such a time as this" to tell others about Him this week in your home, your friendships and your school?

Your home

_____

_____

_____

_____

_____

Your friendships

_____

_____

_____

_____

_____

Your school

_____

_____

_____

_____

_____

5. What might you lose if you tell others about Him?

_____

_____

_____

_____

6. Knowing what you might lose, why should you speak up?

reflect

The life of Esther demonstrates God's power to use us in our current circumstances to tell others about Him. Esther was able to use her position as queen to ask the king to save the Jewish people. Her cousin Mordecai challenged her in Esther 4:14 that she had come to her royal position "for such a time as this." Yet in bringing her request to the king, Esther made a difficult and brave choice (see Esther 4:16). At times, being used by God means making a tough choice. That choice can have a tremendous influence on others.

1. Looking back at your life so far, what is one choice you have made that has had an impact on others?

2. What impact did that choice make on your own life?

3. How would your life be different if you had not made that choice?

4. What unique characteristics do you have that God might want to use to help others know Him?

5. How can you cultivate an awareness of God's timing and the choices He wants you to make?

_____

_____

_____

_____

_____

_____

meditation

Each one should use whatever gift he has
received to serve others, faithfully administering
God's grace in its various forms.

1 PETER 4:10

job:
when the going
gets tough

*Now faith is being sure of what we hope for and certain of what
we do not see. And without faith it is impossible to please God,
because anyone who comes to him must believe that
he exists and that he rewards those who earnestly seek him.*

HEBREWS 11:1,6

What are you doing right now that you could not do without the
help of our supernatural God? When we think of the word
"faith," we often think of the most incredible miracles we've ever
heard about. I don't know about you, but I believe in those kinds
of miracles of faith. Sometimes God chooses to heal a person
who has cancer. In fact, I've even heard of God supernaturally giving a van extra gas mileage when a group of people were smug-

gling Bibles into a country where Bibles were forbidden. There are other times when people have just as much faith, but God chooses not to heal or do a miracle.

Faith is demonstrated by ordinary people doing extraordinary things through the power of God in their lives. Faith is Bob Wieland walking across America on his hands because he has no feet! Faith is Rachel deciding not to abort her baby even though her boyfriend presses her to "get it taken care of." Faith is Cheryl and Hank almost going all the way but deciding to remain virgins, even when they would really like to have sexual intercourse. Faith is Ted choosing not to cheat on exams anymore.

Faith is ordinary people being obedient even when it is hard. It's deciding to not drink or not to have sex before marriage even when "everyone else" is doing it. It's walking away from riches because God is calling you to be a missionary. Faith is asking God to help you overcome an eating disorder or to love the unlovable. Faith is placing all that you are, all that you can be and all that you do into the hands of God.

Faith is doing something or being someone that you could not do or be without the help of our supernatural God.

What are you doing in faith right now? Take a moment and ask God to make you an ordinary person doing extraordinary things for Him.

One person plus God is always a majority.
HOWARD HENDRICKS

job:
when the going
gets tough

starter

TOUGH STUFF: Take a look at the list below and circle which one you think is tougher. When you're done, talk about your choices and your reasons with the whole group.

Outdoor yard work	Indoor housework
A broken arm	A broken leg
An awful haircut	Awful acne
Losing $50	Losing your school ID card
Changing to a new school	Changing to a new church
Failing a class	Getting cut from a sports team

Note: You can download this group study guide in 8¹/₂" x 11" format at **www.gospellight.com/uncommon/the_old_testament.zip.**

Now make a list of all the things in your life that you're grateful for. Maybe a few great friends make the list, or your family, or your iPod. You've got two minutes . . . go!

Now look at the list below and cross off every item that also appears on your list above.

Friends   Musical abilities
Family   Sports abilities
Boyfriend/girlfriend   House
Good grades   Food
Job   Money
Car, bike, skateboard   Church youth group
Driver's license   Physical health
Clothes   Mental health

Anything left? Cross those off, too. You've got nothin'.

message

Imagine you have just lost everything—your family, your friends, your possessions—and you have an extremely painful skin rash. You have the chance to write a letter to God letting Him know how you feel and asking Him any questions you want. Do this on your own, and then share with the group (if you feel comfortable doing so).

Dear God, I feel . . .

_____

_____

_____

_____

_____

_____

_____

My questions are . . .

_____

_____

_____

_____

_____

_____

_____

Love, _____

Today we're going to get to know a guy who lost everything: Job. (Yeah, his name looks like "job," the work you do for a paycheck at the end of the week, but it rhymes with "lobe.") Get together with a partner or small group and crack open your Bibles to find out what happened and how Job handled it.

1. For each of the verses below, describe what happened to Job in your own words.

Job 1:13-15

_____

_____

_____

_____

_____

_____

Job 1:16

_____

_____

_____

_____

_____

Job 1:17

_____

_____

_____

_____

_____

_____

Job 1:18-19

_____

_____

_____

_____

_____

_____

_____

Job 2:7-8

_____

_____

_____

_____

_____

2. At what point would you have screamed, "Enough is enough!"?

_____

_____

_____

_____

_____

_____

3. Job was surrounded by people who meant well, but nonetheless gave some bad advice. Summarize the advice of each friend in your own words and evaluate its effectiveness.

Job's wife (Job 2:9)

Eliphaz (Job 4:8)

Bildad (Job 8:6)

Zophar (Job 20:3-5,27-29)

_____

_____

_____

_____

_____

_____

Elihu (Job 37:23-24)

_____

_____

_____

_____

_____

dig

In many ways, what happened to Job according to the Old Testament resembles what happened to C. S. Lewis, author of *The Chronicles of Narnia* and many other popular Christian books. Job's incredible emotional and intellectual wrestling with God echo a quote from C. S. Lewis: "God whispers to us in our joy and shouts to us in our pain."

C. S. Lewis knew about pain. He was a well-known British professor, theologian and author who had a famous speaking and writing ministry. Upon meeting one of his admirers, Joy, he fell in love with her and they married. Tragically, soon after they were married, Joy died of cancer. Truly, C. S. Lewis experienced deep pain—and only by experiencing that pain did he come to know God's power to comfort and heal.

1. Review Job 13:15. What do you think Job would want to say to C. S. Lewis?

    _____

    _____

    _____

    _____

    _____

    _____

2. What do you think C. S. Lewis would want to say to Job?

    _____

    _____

    _____

    _____

    _____

3. What has been the toughest time in your life so far?

    _____

    _____

    _____

    _____

    _____

    _____

4. How did you relate to God through the tough time?

_____

_____

_____

_____

_____

_____

5. Was your faith strengthened or weakened when the tough time was over?

_____

_____

_____

_____

_____

apply

If one of your non-Christian friends asked you the following questions, how would you respond?

1. Why do bad things happen to good people?

_____

_____

_____

_____

_____

2. Why do good things happen to bad people?

_____

_____

_____

_____

_____

_____

3. Is God fair? Why or why not?

_____

_____

_____

_____

_____

_____

reflect

More than a century ago, Horatio G. Spafford said goodbye to his wife and four daughters as they boarded a ship that was to cross the Atlantic Ocean. To the dismay of Horatio and hundreds of others, the ship went down. There were few survivors.

Horatio's wife was one of those few. She sent her husband the following telegraph that began with the words, "Saved alone." Horatio then sailed to England to rejoin his wife. On the way, he wrote the following powerful and poignant text. His words have become one of the most frequently sung hymns today:

When peace like a river attendeth my way,
When sorrows like sea billows roll;
Whatever my lot, Thou hast taught me to say,
"It is well, it is well with my soul."

1. What area in your life is tough for you right now?

_____
_____
_____
_____
_____
_____
_____
_____

2. What can you do about it?

_____
_____
_____
_____
_____
_____

3. Spend some time in prayer now, bringing before God the
   trial you are facing. Be as honest as you can about your
   fear or anger, and then wait in silence for a few moments.
   See if you are able to pray, "It is well with my soul because . . ." If you are not able to do so yet, commit to

spending 10 minutes a day in prayer during the next week, seeking God's peace.

meditation

Even though I walk through the valley of the shadow of death, I will fear no evil, for you are with me; your rod and your staff, they comfort me.

PSALM 23:4

daniel: standing up and standing out

*I looked for a man [or woman] among them who would
build up the wall and stand before me in the gap on behalf of the
land so I would not have to destroy it, but I found none.*

EZEKIEL 22:30

Imagine for a moment being in Ezekiel's shoes—I mean sandals!
You hear the voice of the living God say that He is looking for
someone to step forward and stand in the gap in order to build
up the crumbled wall of Jerusalem. But God can't find anyone
who has the courage to take on the task.

What would you do if God spoke to you and said He was
looking for a man or a woman who could stand in the gap on behalf of today's youth? Are you willing to be in the minority of

adults who will work with students for the living God? Our society is crumbling around us and the enemy is well-armed and well-funded, but on your side is the living Lord who cares deeply about the society in which His children now reside. God needs to borrow a voice, a loving and caring arm, or perhaps some hands and feet to help reach this generation of young people. Why He would use someone like you and me is a complete mystery to me, but He still chooses to build His kingdom with us less-than-perfect types. In fact, He tells us in His Word that He will supply the life-changing power and all you have to do is stand in the gap.

So let's review: Just like in the days of Ezekiel, the world around us is crumbling and God is looking for ordinary people to do the most extraordinary task of standing in the gap for Him. He'll do the supernatural work, but He still needs a willing body. He offers you and me the same call He issued to Isaiah. Remember when Isaiah said, "Then I heard the voice of the Lord saying, 'Whom shall I send? And who will go for us?'" Do you remember Isaiah's response? It's the same response God is looking for today: "Here am I. Send me!" And God responded, "Go and tell this people" (Isaiah 6:8-9).

When we think of people like Isaiah and Ezekiel, we probably imagine larger-than-life personalities—the superstars of their day. But I'm beginning to think that they were even more ordinary in looks and brains than everybody else; what made them stand out was an uncompromising commitment to take a stand for God.

So what about you?

I am willing to go anywhere and do anything for Jesus Christ.
DAVE HESS, 17-YEAR-OLD SUMMER MISSIONARY

daniel: standing up and standing out

starter

UNDER THE INFLUENCE. Who would you listen to in the following areas? Check the box of the person from whom you would accept advice.

	Friends	Parents	Myself
What to wear to school	❑	❑	❑
What movie to see Saturday	❑	❑	❑
What radio station to listen to	❑	❑	❑
How to get the attention of a girl/guy you like	❑	❑	❑
What to believe about God	❑	❑	❑
How to handle a fight with a friend	❑	❑	❑

Note: You can download this group study guide in 8$\frac{1}{2}$" x 11" format at **www.gospellight.com/uncommon/the_old_testament.zip.**

Overall, who would you listen to the most? _____

Now look at the list of freedoms below and check the three (and only three!) that are most important to you—so important to you that you would stand up for that freedom even if you were opposed by all of your friends. Then discuss the following questions with the whole group.

- ❑ The freedom to eat whatever you want
- ❑ The freedom to drive
- ❑ The freedom to choose your own friends
- ❑ The freedom to go to church
- ❑ The freedom to keep your room as you want it
- ❑ The freedom to listen to whatever music you want
- ❑ The freedom to begin a Bible club on your campus
- ❑ The freedom to pray

1. Picture yourself in a class debate in which you are the only one who stands for your three chosen freedoms. How would you feel?

_____

_____

_____

_____

_____

_____

2. What would you say?

_____

_____

_____

_____

3. What would prevent you from simply giving in to the majority opinion?

_____

_____

_____

_____

_____

message

As a young man, Daniel was ripped away from his home in Jerusalem and taken in captivity to Babylon. In this new and hostile land, Daniel repeatedly chose to stand up for his convictions, even when no one else stood with him. By taking such bold stands, he quickly stood out from the rest.

In the study below, you'll see that Daniel stood out in three ways:

1. In *purity*, by avoiding harmful influences
2. In *integrity*, by doing the right thing
3. In *godliness*, by following God no matter what

With a partner, look up the following verses. In your own words, describe how Daniel stood up for the Lord *and* how he stood out from the crowd. Keep in mind Daniel's *purity, integrity* and *godliness*.

1. Daniel 1:1-14

    How Daniel stood up for God:

    _____

    _____

    _____

    _____

    _____

    How Daniel stood out from the crowd:

    _____

    _____

    _____

    _____

    _____

2. Daniel 1:15-17

    How Daniel stood up for God:

    _____

    _____

    _____

    _____

    _____

How Daniel stood out from the crowd:

_____

_____

_____

_____

3. Daniel 6:1-2,4-5

How Daniel stood up for God:

_____

_____

_____

_____

How Daniel stood out from the crowd:

_____

_____

_____

_____

4. Daniel 6:3-4

How Daniel stood up for God:

_____

_____

_____

_____

How Daniel stood out from the crowd:

5. Daniel 6:7-11

How Daniel stood up for God:

How Daniel stood out from the crowd:

6. Daniel 6:21-23

How Daniel stood up for God:

_____

_____

_____

_____

_____

How Daniel stood out from the crowd:

_____

_____

_____

_____

dig

Discuss the following questions with your partner.

1. Why was King Darius so distraught according to Daniel 6:11-20?

_____

_____

_____

_____

_____

2. How do you think Daniel felt after being thrown into the lions' den as it became dark and the lions began to growl in hunger?

3. How did Daniel's commitment to standing for the Lord benefit the kingdom according to Daniel 6:26-27?

4. Do you believe that Daniel thought God would protect him in the lions' den? Why or why not?

5. Does God guarantee us protection when we take risky stands for Him? How do you know?

_____

_____

_____

_____

_____

_____

_____

6. If taking a stand for God is no guarantee of protection, why should we stand up for Him at all?

_____

_____

_____

_____

_____

_____

_____

apply

On your own, take a few minutes to describe how you can stand up for the Lord and stand out from the crowd in purity, integrity and godliness.

1. I can stand for the Lord in each of these areas this week by . . .

Purity:

Integrity:

Godliness:

2. How will taking these stands cause you to stand out from the crowd?

3. What negative consequences might you face for your decisions?

4. Given this possibility, are you still ready to take a stand this week? Why or why not?

reflect

Although it may seem like you're on your own when it comes to peer pressure, you really aren't alone. Every adult you know faced significant pressure from their friends growing up—in fact, they may face peer pressure from their friends now! This week, sit down with a parent, youth leader or other adult whom you respect and interview him or her about the pressures he or she has experienced.

1. What specific pressures did you face when you were a teenager?

    ....

    ....

    ....

    ....

    ....

    ....

    ....

2. What peer pressure do you face now, either at home, at work or in the neighborhood?

    ....

    ....

    ....

    ....

    ....

    ....

    ....

3. Do you think today's peer pressure is stronger, weaker or the same as when you were my age?

_____

_____

_____

_____

_____

_____

4. Why do you think teenagers are more likely to listen to their friends or the media than to their parents or church?

_____

_____

_____

_____

_____

_____

5. What helps you stand up for the right thing?

_____

_____

_____

_____

_____

_____

_____

6. In what ways can you help me stand up for the Lord, even under pressure?

_____

_____

_____

_____

_____

_____

_____

Spend some time in prayer together, asking God for His strength and guidance as you both seek to stand strong for Him.

meditation

Be on your guard; stand firm in the faith;

be men [and women] of courage; be strong.

1 CORINTHIANS 16:13

HOME WORD

WHERE PARENTS GET REAL ANSWERS

Get Equipped with HomeWord...

LISTEN
HomeWord Radio
programs reach over 800 communities nationwide with *HomeWord with Jim Burns* – a daily ½ hour interview feature, *HomeWord Snapshots* – a daily 1 minute family drama, and *HomeWord this Week* – a ½ hour weekend edition of the daily program, and our one-hour program.

CLICK
HomeWord.com
provides advice and resources to millions of visitors each year. A truly interactive website, HomeWord.com provides access to parent newsletter, Q&As, online broadcasts, tip sheets, our online store and more.

READ
HomeWord Resources
parent newsletters, equip families and Churches worldwide with practical Q&As, online broadcasts, tip sheets, our online store and more. Many of these resources are also packaged digitally to meet the needs of today's busy parents.

ATTEND
HomeWord Events
Understanding Your Teenager, Building Healthy Morals & Values, Generation 2 Generation and Refreshing Your Marriage are held in over 100 communities nationwide each year. HomeWord events educate and encourage parents while providing answers to life's most pressing parenting and family questions.

A Ministry with *Jim Burns*

In response to the overwhelming needs of parents and families, Jim Burns founded HomeWord in 1985. HomeWord, a Christian organization, equips and encourages parents, families, and churches worldwide.

Find Out More

Sign up for our FREE daily
e-devotional and parent e-newsletter
at HomeWord.com, or call 800.397.9725.

HomeWord.com

Small Group Curriculum Kits

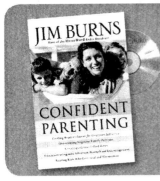

Confident Parenting Kit

This is a must-have resource for today's family! Let Jim Burns help you to tackle overcrowded lives, negative family patterns, while creating a grace-filled home and raising kids who love God and themselves.

Kit contains:
- 6 sessions on DVD featuring Dr. Jim Burns
- CD with reproducible small group leader's guide and participant guides
- poster, bulletin insert, and more

Creating an Intimate Marriage Kit

Dr. Jim Burns wants every couple to experience a marriage filled with A.W.E.: affection, warmth, and encouragement. He shows husbands and wives how to make their marriage a priority as they discover ways to repair the past, communicate and resolve conflict, refresh their marriage spiritually, and more!

Kit contains:
- 6 sessions on DVD featuring Dr. Jim Burns
- CD with reproducible small group leader's guide and participant guides
- poster, bulletin insert, and more

Parenting Teenagers for Positive Results

This popular resource is designed for small groups and Sunday schools. The DVD features real family situations played out in humorous family vignettes followed by words of wisdom by youth and family expert, Jim Burns, Ph.D.

Kit contains:
- 6 sessions on DVD featuring Dr. Jim Burns
- CD with reproducible small group leader's guide and participant guides
- poster, bulletin insert, and more

Teaching Your Children Healthy Sexuality Kit

Trusted family authority Dr. Jim Burns outlines a simple and practical guide for parents on how to develop in their children a healthy perspective regarding their bodies and sexuality. Promotes godly values about sex and relationships.

Kit contains:
- 6 sessions on DVD featuring Dr. Jim Burns
- CD with reproducible small group leader's guide and participant guides
- poster, bulletin insert, and more

Tons of helpful resources for youth workers, parents and youth. Visit our online store at www.HomeWord.com or call us at 800-397-9725

HOME WORD
WHERE PARENTS GET REAL ANSWERS

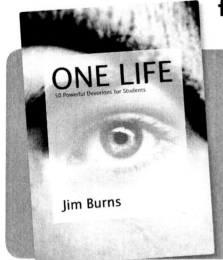

Small Group Curriculum Kits

Confirming Your Faith Kit

Rite-of-Passage curriculum empowers youth to make wise decisions...to choose Christ. Help them take ownership of their faith! Lead them to do this by experiencing a vital Christian lifestyle.

Kit contains:
- 13 engaging lessons
- Ideas for retreats and special Celebration
- Solid foundational Bible concepts
- 1 leaders guide and 6 student journals (booklets)

10 Building Blocks Kit

Learn to live, laugh, love, and play together as a family. When you learn the 10 essential principles for creating a happy, close-knit household, you'll discover a family that shines with love for God and one another! Use this curriculum to help equip families in your church.

Kit contains:
- 10 sessions on DVD featuring Dr. Jim Burns
- CD with reproducible small group leader's guide and participant guides
- poster and bulletin insert
- 10 Building Blocks book

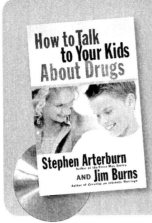

How to Talk to Your Kids About Drugs Kit

Dr. Jim Burns speaks to parents about the important topic of talking to their kids about drugs. You'll find everything you need to help parents learn and implement a plan for drug-proofing their kids.

Kit contains:
- 2 session DVD featuring family expert Dr. Jim Burns
- CD with reproducible small group leader's guide and participant guides
- poster, bulletin insert, and more
- How to Talk to Your Kids About Drugs book

Tons of helpful resources for youth workers, parents and youth. Visit our online store at www.HomeWord.com or call us at 800-397-9725

HOME WORD
WHERE PARENTS GET REAL ANSWERS

also available from
jim burns

resisting temptation
Jim Burns, General Editor
ISBN 978.08307.47894
ISBN 08307.47893

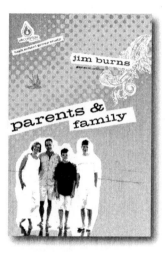

parents & family
Jim Burns, General Editor
ISBN 978.08307.50979
ISBN 08307.50975

prayer & the devotional life
Jim Burns, General Editor
ISBN 978.08307.54793
ISBN 08307.54792

the new testament
Jim Burns, General Editor
ISBN 978.08307.55660
ISBN 08307.55667

uncommon

uncommon
leaders' resources

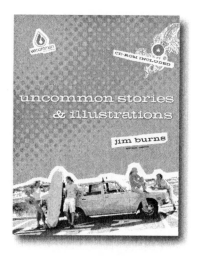

uncommon stories
& illustration
Jim Burns, General Editor
ISBN 978.08307.47252
ISBN 08307.47257

uncommon dramas,
skits & sketches
Jim Burns, General Editor
ISBN 978.08307.47917
ISBN 08307.47915

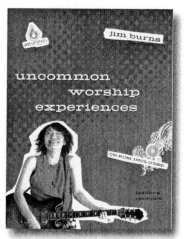

uncommon object lessons
& discussion starters
Jim Burns, General Editor
ISBN 978.08307.50986
ISBN 08307.50983

uncommon worship
experiences
Jim Burns, General Editor
ISBN 978.08307.54830
ISBN 08307.54830